Since 1975, El Arroyo has been serving up Tex-Mex with a side of laughs on our famous marquee sign that stands on the corner of West 5th and Campbell in Austin, Texas. The Last Queso Stop Before a Bunch of Yoga Studios - over the years we've covered every food pun imaginable while never forgetting witty commentary on current events. The face(s) behind the daily marquee messages remains a secret for now... But we're always happy to take submissions from customers and internet fans. Thanks to you, the buyer of this book, and all of our followers - thanks for smiling. We hope to bring you years of smiles to come!

Cheers,
El Arroyo

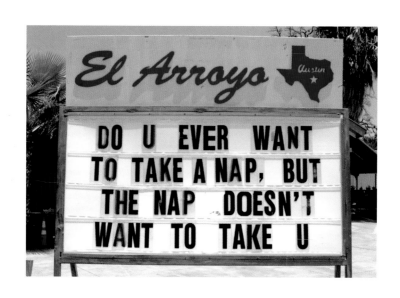

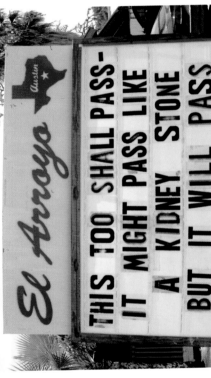

5

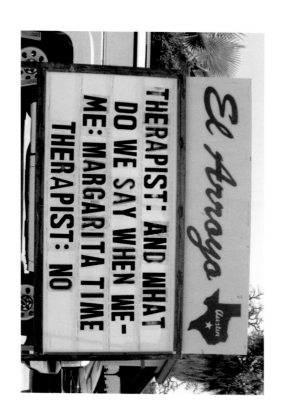

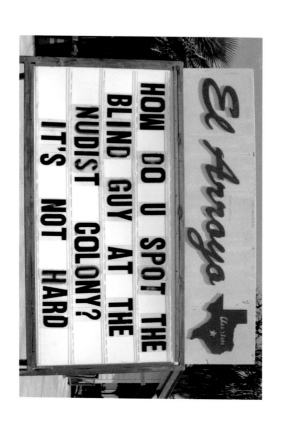

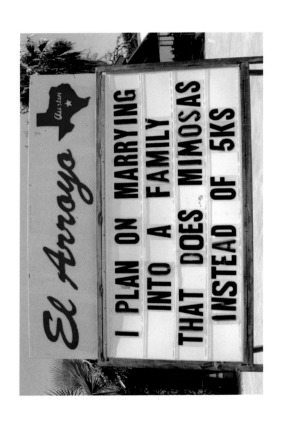

El Arroyo

Austin

WHY CAN'T A
CHAMELEON CHANGE
HIS COLORS?
A REPTILE DYSFUNCTION

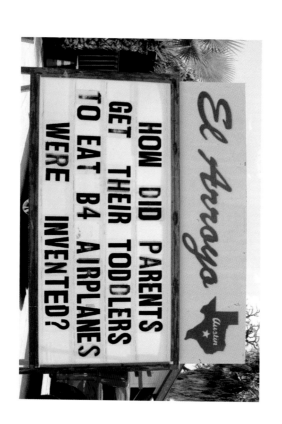

El Arroyo

DO TWINS
EVER REALIZE
THAT ONE OF THEM
WAS UNPLANNED?

I WAS GOING TO TELL A TIME TRAVELING JOKE BUT YOU GUYS DIDN'T LIKE IT

El Arroyo

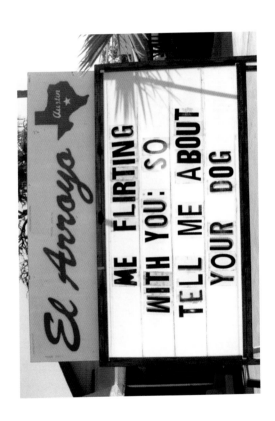

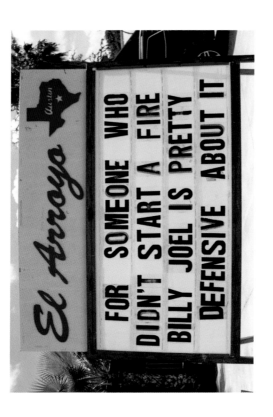

FOR SOMEONE WHO DIDN'T START A FIRE BILLY JOEL IS PRETTY DEFENSIVE ABOUT IT

El Arroyo
Austin
LISTEN I STILL
WANT TO BE
INVITED BUT
I'M NOT COMING

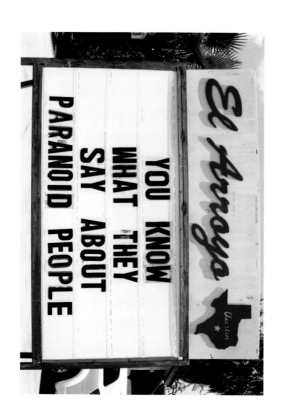

TO THE PERSON THAT STOLE MY ANTIDEPRESSANTS, I HOPE YOU'RE HAPPY NOW

IT'S OK IF U FALL
APART SOMETIMES
TACOS FALL APART
& WE STILL LOVE THEM

73

HAVING A KID IS LIKE HAVING A BROKE LITTLE BEST FRIEND WHO THINKS UR RICH

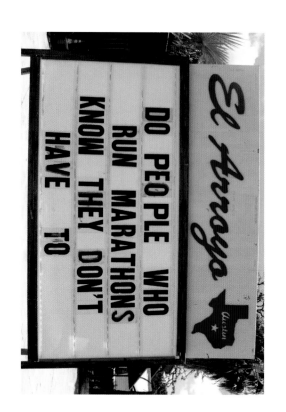

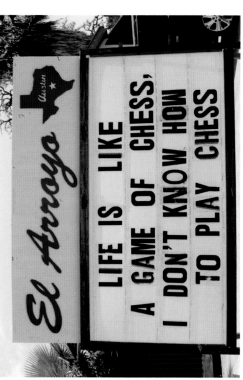

ISBN 978-1-7327026-5-3

Library of Congress Control Number: 2018910612

Some characters and events in this book are fictitious. Any similarity to real persons, living or dead, is coincidental and not intended by the author.

Editing by Paige Winstanley
Front cover image by Paige Winstanley
All photographs by Cozumel Publishing Company, LLC
Book design by Cozumel Publishing Company, LLC

Printed and bound in the USA
First Printing August 2020
Published by Cozumel Publishing Company, LLC
P.O. Box 50550
Austin, TX, USA 78763

Visit www.elarroyo.com

Facebook: /elarroyoatx
Instagram: @elarroyo_atx
Twitter: @elarroyo_atx